Carpe
Demons

Scott Alexander Jones

2014 Unsolicited Press Trade Paperback Edition
Copyright © 2014 Scott Alexander Jones
All Rights Reserved.
Published in the United States by Unsolicited Press.

ISBN: 0692240802
ISBN-13: 978069224080

Contents

1

2

3

4

5

6

7

8

9

10

11

12

13

14

15

16

17

18

19

20

kat•su [kät'soō] exclamation
a sharp cry used by a Zen teacher and pupil
at the moment of enlightenment.

For over sixty years
I often cried Katsu! *to no avail.*
And now, while dying,
Once more to cry Katsu!
Won't change a thing.

—Kokei Sochin

January 17, 1597

Poems

Past
The past

Tensing
Of muscles

& names
By heart

I'm absorbing
Bonfires along the beach

Only enough to say
We won't retain any of this—

A plague of eggs
For ancient me

Pensive with fuzzy
Wisdom. Just try & weave

Homespun scriptures
From floating ash, you sad

Piece of shit,
Starting with this

Wind
Strewn

Star
Lit

Sand
Dune—

The liar in me
Might say I'm fine

Or I'm fine dying
Or I'm fine dying here

Indoors, surrounded by mallets of rain
You tell the rusty taste

Of skeleton
Keys lingering in your throat—

The genocide of closely mown lawns
Is rarely too Renaissance

To vote a straight secessionist ticket—
Enough already.

We get it.

You've got a skull.
I've got a skull.

All those Jane & John
Doe's, scattered in catacombs

As the silk waters begin to rise—
Try & get some sleep—

Feed & remember
Me to the ladies

When steam billows up
Thru the city's teeth—

Crows feet spider
Web the edges of your eyes

At last, fracturing like ice
Only slow like hideous

Car wrecks seconds before impact—
The here

& now is still
Indistinct as the difference between

Cultivating beards
& forgetting to shave—

Ketchup stains on tattered pea coats
Last forever, as in last

November & you swear by next
Diem you'll carpe

The semen out of it
The way we say the dead

Of winter
& winter

Turns us into evergreens, brings us
Crawling from flooded cellars

& bastards like us naked
First harnessed fire

& the dance that night
Must've been like

The end of the world.

When the copper Camaro
Accordions into origami

The windows are Dickensian with fog—
The Phoenician pirates

Genuflect into ambitious pretzels—
Mudras worthy of Kama Sutras—

Don't be that wounded soldier crawling topless
Into the snowstorm—

Don't abandon your marinara newborn—
Sentient rigatoni

Cancerous with cheddar,
Your remains are everglades here shortly,

Having slid impassively thru the bowels
Of a God who loves you enough

To never come into existence
Or the Texas hill country

With immaculate birth
Certificates, screaming sorry

About the holocaust, the atom
Bomb. It's like I've just woken

Into a coma.

More than death
The smell of death

Really the thought
Of smelling death,

Which I've never
Smelled, terrifies me

Shitless like the shit
That leaves us

When you're not here
To apprentice entrails

About restraint
Or say morning

Fog across the valley
Below Timberline Lodge

Or point down
& say nothing—

The hum of the refrigerator
≠ coyotes

& wind, so let's pretend
We are Alexandrian

Shipbuilders & so what if the coastlines can't last—
They've only got American flag

Stamps at the post office. The American poet
Stamps were discontinued last fall & all

That comes to mind is: *I'm fine*
With whatever.

If prayer's cowering in my parietal
Lobe, I'm mostly parroting how I'd kill

To stare into the yellowshot
Eyes of an ice

Age
Ape

Man 800
Grandfathers ago

& debate rainfall on ferns & not
Say machine

Guns or I'm so
So sorry.

When I say I'd kill
I mean I am killing

Time, mindless
As Bodhidharma—

I am dying
To scuff my feet

On the elephant
Rug for weeks, Tesla

Coils humming, polygraphs
Interrogating my testicles—

I'd kill to see who killed who
Among my ancestry—

Roman men slitting the throats of the
Roman men they blow—

Who cares if they go by Flavius
& vow: we are the sea

Merchants, the sheepherders, who cares?
I'd kill to extend my hand to

The nothing & the dust
Mites in the attic—

I am dying to kill the dance
Lights & go: *Let's dance*

The Lindy Hop
Till the emphysema takes us

You miserable silver fox.

The day you took your life
Into your own hands

By not taking your life
You kept hearing dial tones

& nobody breathing over the phone—
Nobody skimming *Time*

For the least glossy toilet paper—
Nobody smelling corpses

Gnarly
& garlanded

& BBQ along the waterfront—
The most exquisite mood

Lighting for the skiffs
You'd ever seen

Of excrement drifting
Toward the simpleminded sea—

Don't say *samsara* just yet or ever—
Say wisps of nothing, yellow as autumn,

Autumnal as toilet stains—
Say chimneys in winter

In Wyoming, which
You've barely driven thru—

With no moon left
To cast our contours

Over the grass & contrast
Us with what is never us

We might be anywhere
Dense & blackly forested—

By frightened men with fire
Arms & fire, I mean

Come on, these woods
Ain't gonna chop themself—

Quitcher bickerin' or else—
In the roofless union hall

After the floods withdrew, there were
Silver ribbons in the rafters

In the wind, which is the empty
Half of breath, you said

& we've got the rest
Of our deaths to sleep

& instead of I trust you
I hissed enough already, be quiet

A minute, we get it. The leaves
Were crinkling under the weight

Of something with feet—

If only it were easy
As pointing at this supercentenarian

Sleeping in the middle of the street—
Her rickety wheelchair.

The redbrick porn theater.
Horse rings in ruptured sidewalk.

We used to be pink seahorses in stomachs
Blinking like the denizens of opium dens—

Rainbow trout readying our mouths
To fellate the oceans

That overwhelm
Us so that nothing's noticeably here—

Jelly donuts never fail
To bubble into macrofocus

On candlelit vigils for hired guns
Yet I don't really like or dislike

Extravagant pastries; they're one
Of the few things

I'm on the fence about.

We'll never leave this world alive
You sing to the pancake

Faced orangutan I've seldom been—
One doesn't prance

By providence up the stairwell of the cotton
Plantation from *Gone with the Wind*

Dousing the banisters in gasoline,
Honeydew, dying aphids—

The feverous children all grew
Swiftly & predictably into root vegetables—

They are howling to the sorceress
Who stirs the suede

Gazpacho they can't swim out of
& the nails in the floorboards are chattering

Away about amber freight trains
Rapidly approaching

With winter teeth—

I can also see myself waitressing
Or blinking amphibiously

As we bludgeon faces made of sludge
Beneath the arctic sky on acid—

We are animals most when lighting candles, maybe—
Mostly when scratching matches in blackouts—

Mannequins if mannequins
Are godlike as infanticide.

Christ, there's only a baker's dozen of us left
From the 1890s & you are pissing

& it hits you, the aloneness of yellow
Dive bar bathroom mirrors—

Dogs can't pour beer without aloha shirts.
Reagan, you swear, has seen this poster.

Dogs made of bone keep unearthing
Dog bones made of dog.

The Victorian doorknob's locked.
Someone outside keeps strangling it.

That diamond sound of water on water
Comes trickling to a halt.

Maggots in the caribou's ribcage,
We apes invented elves—

Every toenail you've clipped
Is somewhere this minute

& by *chameleon* I mean
The boa constrictor

Can barely fit thru the train tunnel—
Sunup brings the trash

Men crooning to our balcony—
A Christmas of wine bottles, jingly & senseless

Save that harem of wilted menthols—
If you've ever seen marionette strings

Made of sausage links
Then you've seen me,

Dear breeders,
In the rumor of a monsoon

Dying to know what snow feels like—

The trashman's howling
& you are shrinking

Back in time like a pea
Green penis in a turtle shell,

Typing *October* into a gadget
From the Dust Bowl—

Tomorrow it's quill pens, then
Papyrus & handprints

For the dying flame—
A dozen words for *naked*—

Graveside words for *nightly*—
The night wakes you from dreams

Of being eaten alive by wolves
To being eaten alive by wolves—

The awfulness is always
Awful as it's always been

& Dadaist
& uncalled for—

The holiest of holy men
Are always grabbing their dicks

& going wah
wah—

According to a report from
The Laurens County Sheriff's Office

A Candler, N.C. woman
Danced before the service,

Waved a wand around the casket,
Opened the lid, laid her hands

On the deceased's head
& struck the body.

Nicole Marie-Loretta Leonard, 25,
Has been charged with disturbing a funeral

& public disorderly conduct
In Tuesday's incident.

Tammy Fausel said she'd never
Seen this woman & had no idea why

She would be at this funeral at the Church of God
On Old Church of God Road.

Everybody was just kind of flabbergasted
She said. *They didn't know what was going on.*

The woman took flowers
From the top of the casket

& showered them over the family
Before leaving in a burgundy

Toyota, according to the report.
When deputies asked her why

She acted the way she did, she said:
It felt like the right thing to do

At the time.

The pugs are shivering
In corduroy sweaters

& the fossil record shits us not
They come from wolves, god

Damn it, there are reasons we grow teeth—
Burn these receipts at breakneck speed

So we won't keep scribbling sweet
Little nothings to the wind in general—

The greatest generation
Of primates in the sky

To bomb the quilted countryside
Could live with fewer inventories of

Avocadoes & nightmares—
Don't take our word for it, please—

Take the zombie on the Baptist placard
Beholding the Nothing

Steadfast & steady
Between sweaty palms—

Love,
Me

(STOP) is how we sign telegrams
(STOP) when it's 1903—

(STOP) How one pleads
With juniper trees

When the only footprints in the ashy woods
Are yours & you are barefoot—

Or the man with Down syndrome & acid
Washed overalls

Is probing his honeycomb
Nose & blinking & so what, what

Ever, licking his fingers & deep down
One should never stare

Dead on into the Void—
Like the sun let it whisper

Its bleak bleakness bleakly
Thru the clearest days of winter—

Repulsive as the pustules
Of jittery teenagers

We'll never see last winter again
No matter how many lasers—

Lend us your impressions on earthquakes
When the world is over,

Dear stockbrokers cast in bronze—
Cobblers fawning for amphetamines—

Pretend it's a century
From whatever now feels like—

All the pretty Tang Dynasty emperors
Can't stop filling ponds with wine

& lynching lambs in bonsai
& trumpeting fuck

Or it's your life
To the naked partygoers—

This exit, you swear, is the
Exit we need as we sail

Past the exit sign, the wine
Fossilizing inside us—

Doomed to prosperity,
Let the bankers keep on reciting

Yeats at holocaustic banquets—
The graveyard's patient

As the landfill & the love
Letters & holey socks you plan

To leave behind reek of vinegar
On the frothy beach—

The fratboys are vomiting into plastic cups
& dozing & shivering & swallowing—

Likewise, the saltwater tides,
Nowhere all the time,

Depending on the whaleness
Of undiscovered drowning victims—

Tonight, let's swim out past the jetty
Like there's no tomorrow

& tomorrow like no tonight
We might arrive at the orgy in the lighthouse

Armed with absinthe & a book
Of matches—

You
Say

You say
Your name

Not like *boll weevil*,
The beetle, but *the devil*,

Dear mentor from another centaur,
Which means nothing

Like gliding thru bodily functions
As the highways grumble with commuters—

Drowning locusts out of Wellington,
I am suffocating my ears with toilet paper—

In the telecast window, blue fire
Crackers blossom in the Chinese New Year

Down by waterfront docks the Kiwis call Oriental
Bay. Molly swears it's cicadas

But we've slept enough
To know they're not the kind

Of ghost that hibernates forever
& everyone & their mother

Always goes on
& on about,

Like where are we going with all this
Quicksand in our shoes?

I am trying to tell you:
I'll be done with my 20s

On Julius Caesar's 2,055th deathday,
Which I'm trying to tell you is soon—

I am trying to say the harvest
Moon = God's glory

Hole. The Milky Way,
a nocturnal emission.

In tonight's wine coma
You are lighting torches

Down catacombs
During the power outage—

I am thirsty enough
To say thirsty as fuck

& you are Rimbaud
The Abyssinian arms dealer

& we are always dying
To evacuate

Our bladders over the nearest balding, birth
Marked skulls, always burning

To leap into lavish banquets
Peopled with people who drive people

In blonde robes
To set themselves aflame—

www.ingramcontent.com/pod-product-compliance
Lightning Source LLC
Chambersburg PA
CBHW022001100426
42738CB00042B/1359